# HAYNES EXPLAINS
# PENSIONERS
## Owners' Workshop Manual

© Haynes Publishing • Written by **Boris Starling**

Published in October 2016
Reprinted in July and December 2017

A catalogue record for this book is available from the British Library

ISBN 978 1 78521 105 8

Haynes Publishing, Sparkford, Yeovil,
Somerset BA22 7JJ, UK
Tel: +44 (0) 1963 440635
Website: www.haynes.com

Haynes North America, Inc.,
859 Lawrence Drive, Newbury Park,
California 91320, USA

Printed and bound in Malaysia

Cover image from Getty Images

Written by **Boris Starling**
Edited by **Louise McIntyre**
Designed by **Richard Parsons**

# Safety first!

As the following report from Dorset Police demonstrates, retirement is no longer the haven of security it once was.

**Dennis Pearce (88)**
– drunk in charge of a mobility scooter, Peverell Avenue West
**Doreen Webster (79)**
– improper storage of knitting needles, Bough Acres Nursing Home
**Leonard Gratton (83)**
– reckless tee drive on the 15th hole, Osmington Mills Golf Club
**Ethel Carlisle (84)**
– attempted BASE jump from the Hardy Monument, Portesham

# Working facilities

Optimum working facilities for the pensioner vary greatly. Some pensioners may find they operate best on c. 75 acres of maintained turf divided into fairways, greens, rough areas, and most importantly an area of ill repute known only as 'the 19th hole.' Others may prefer a large indoor arena where all attention is on a man in a cheap tuxedo and wearing too much hair pomade who utters strange phrases such as 'man alive', 'key in the door' and 'two fat ladies'.

# Contents

# Introduction

Welcome to HAYNES EXPLAINS: PENSIONERS. Retirement: when you stop living at work and begin working at life. Those are the traditional views of being a pensioner. But of all the topics covered in this HAYNES EXPLAINS series, retirement is – perhaps ironically – the one that is changing quickest of all.

Retirement is definitely not what it used to be. For a start, retirement age is getting later and later as people live longer (and government budgets creak ever more loudly). The average Joe who thinks he might retire at 65 nowadays does some quick financial planning and realises he can live comfortably for 12 minutes, give or take.

People retire later. They retire in stages. They do more in retirement than they used to. Heck, some do more in retirement than they used to at work. Not so long ago, retirement was basically doing nothing without worrying that someone would catch you at it, and you could pretty much guarantee never coming across a pensioner as long as you stayed away from golf courses and bingo halls.

Now pensioners are everywhere: doing triathlons, throwing themselves out of planes (come on, guys, Ryanair's not that bad), and in Donald Trump's case even running for President. The grey army is on the march.

# About this manual

The aim of this manual is to help you get the best value from your retirement. It can do this in several ways. It can help you (a) decide what work must be done and (b) tackle this work yourself, though you may choose to have much of it performed by external contractors such as That Nice Young Man From The Village, The Carer Who Talks Too Much or The Curtain Twitcher Across The Road.

The manual has drawings and descriptions to show the function and layout of the various components. Tasks are described in a logical order so that even a novice can do the work, which should prove useful if you've forgotten exactly what it was you asked or if you did spell it out, you know you did, but young people nowadays never listen do they and are always on their phones aren't they?

#  Dimensions, weights and capacities

## Retirement home
Available rooms ......................................................... 44
Staff ........................................................................... 26

## Residents
Blokes who keep going on about the war............. 4
Women who could cover Wembley in knitting..... 13
Ones with family who never visit........................... 7
Members of champion quiz team ......................... 4
Bribes offered to quizmaster to fix next quiz ...... £75

## Kerb weight
Mobility scooter and shopping, fully laden .......... 450kg

## Maximum speed and acceleration
Mobility scooter, downhill with following wind .... 0–8mph in 30 seconds.
Lateral G-force (while slaloming) ......................... 1.5

## Engine
Bore ........................................................................ Malcolm in the corner, always
................................................................................. going on about how NASA
................................................................................. faked the moon landing
Stroke ..................................................................... An ever-present risk, unfortunately
Power...................................................................... To the people. The older the better
Torque ..................................................................... Affected by arthritis
Redline .................................................................... When the electricity goes off
................................................................................. in the middle of *Countdown*

## Price
OTR price ................................................................ Paid my taxes for 40 years, sonny
Depreciation ........................................................... Gradual but inexorable

# Prepping the vehicle

When you finally leave work, make sure you have a party. Parties mark almost all rites of passage in modern life – school leaving, 18th birthdays, 21st birthdays, graduation, wedding, new home, birthdays that end with '0', divorce, second wedding and so on. Most of these will have been rather better than the warm white wine, tasteless canapés and insincere speech from your managing director (and if they weren't, that doesn't say much for your friends).

*So go wild...* tell your colleagues exactly what you think of them. Get hog-whimperingly drunk. Basically treat it like an office Christmas party with one added bonus: they'll all have to come into work tomorrow, but you won't. Though they may wish you'd been this lively when you were actually working there rather than saving the best till last.

*...then* – once your hangover's cleared, of course, which at your age might take the best part of a week, as let's face it you're not getting any younger, grandpa, which is after all why you're here in the first place – be prepared to feel a little dazed and disorientated. The more competitive and assertive you've been at work, the harder you'll find it to switch off.

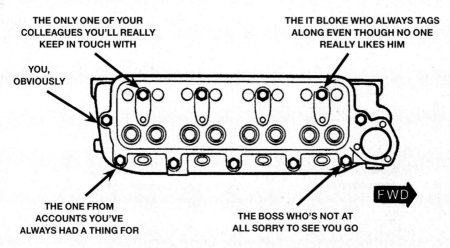

THE ONLY ONE OF YOUR COLLEAGUES YOU'LL REALLY KEEP IN TOUCH WITH

THE IT BLOKE WHO ALWAYS TAGS ALONG EVEN THOUGH NO ONE REALLY LIKES HIM

YOU, OBVIOUSLY

THE ONE FROM ACCOUNTS YOU'VE ALWAYS HAD A THING FOR

THE BOSS WHO'S NOT AT ALL SORRY TO SEE YOU GO

FWD

FIG 4•1 **MUSICAL CHAIRS – PLANNING THE SEATING AT YOUR FAREWELL DO**

#  Advantages of being a pensioner

| Good news | Bad news |
|---|---|
| Free public transport | You'll forget where you're going |
| You'll probably be released first in a hostage situation | The shock might have finished you off by then |
| You have almost nothing left to learn the hard way | Everything you've learnt has been the hard way |
| You and your friends love to discuss operations | The operations in question are mainly yours |
| You'll have to buy fewer things | Those things are increasingly likely to outlast you |
| Politics don't rouse you to argument so much any more | Pension plans do |
| You can live without sex | You can't live without glasses |
| Your joints are better weather forecasters than anyone on TV | Your joints won't let you move fast enough to escape the bad weather |
| Your vision won't get much worse | You're not exactly starting from eagle territory as it is anymore |
| Your hearing won't get much worse | I SAID YOUR HEARING WON'T GET MUCH WORSE |
| You make use of your health insurance | Your premiums reflect this |
| You no longer regard speed limits as a recommended minimum | Unfortunately everyone else on the road does |
| You can throw a party without the neighbours complaining | Because all the guests forgot they were supposed to turn up |
| Your secrets are safe with your friends | They can't remember them either |
| You've got all the time in the world to sit down | Your piles have got other ideas |

# Shock absorbers

The first weeks or months of retirement can be like losing your virginity, planning a big night out with friends or a World Cup Final: the anticipation is often better than the reality.

What is a seismic change for you is also one for your wife too. Whether she works or not, she may have a more established domestic social circle, and having you around all the time under her feet isn't necessarily an unqualified bonus as far as she's concerned. She will tell you this, either in plain English or in a series of sighs which are in their own way as differentiated and eloquent as all those Eskimo words for different types of snow.

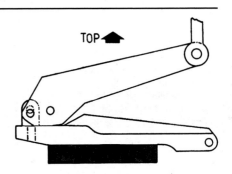

TOP

FIG 4•2 **JUST WHEN YOU THOUGHT IT WAS SAFE TO GO BACK IN THE HOUSE...**

**Every evening she looks pleased when you say 'Honey, I'm home.' Until the evening you add 'forever'.**

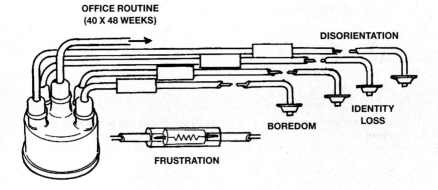

OFFICE ROUTINE
(40 X 48 WEEKS)

DISORIENTATION

BOREDOM

IDENTITY LOSS

FRUSTRATION

FIG 4•3 **THE LIFE TRANSFORMER – FROM WORK TO REST**

# ⚠️ Retirement

| What you think retirement will be like | What retirement is actually like |
| --- | --- |
| Your wife will be thrilled to see you | You will get under your wife's feet |
| You'll have all day to do things | You'll be bored rigid by midday |
| You'll sleep late every morning | Your body clock will wake you at dawn |
| You'll play lots of golf | Your golfing buddies have got lives too |
| You can take the grandkids to the zoo | The grandkids are glued to their PS4 |
| You'll take endless mini-breaks in interesting eastern European cities | You'll spend 10 hours in Gdansk airport waiting for a delayed flight |
| You won't miss work at all | You will miss work. Quite a bit. |
| You'll pop into the office to see all your old colleagues now and then | If you're not billable time, they're not interested |
| You'll make lots of new friends | The supermarket checkout staff will chat to you. Only at slow times. |
| You'll still be in your PJs at lunchtime | No you won't. You're not Hugh Hefner. |
| You'll feel free and liberated | You'll feel a little lost and rootless |
| You'll read all the classic novels you never had time for | You'll read *Golf Monthly*, *Classic Car* and the *Radio Times* |
| You'll watch all the classic movies you never had time for | You'll watch *Countdown*, the *Jeremy Kyle Show* and old *Top Gear* |
| You'll fix up an old car from scratch | You'll get as far as buying the Haynes Manual for said car |
| You'll go wild fishing on a remote Norwegian fjord | You'll set up your rod on the local riverbank and promptly fall asleep |
| You'll catch up with people you haven't seen in years | You'll soon realise why you haven't seen them in years |
| You'll run for office | You'll lie down until the urge passes |

# Regenerative braking

Type the word 'tired' into Google and one of the first autocomplete suggestions you'll get is 'all the time'. Most jobs are demanding, either physically, mentally or both, and the older you get the less able you are to maintain such a punishing pace, at least not without recourse to one form of pharmaceutical aid or another.

You could be forgiven for thinking that only a complete stop will do. But rapid deceleration can lead to cold turkey almost as bad as that experienced by Ewan McGregor's character in *Trainspotting*. Instead, try slowing down gradually, so you're on a glide path rather than a hard stop.

You've still got a long way to go before the three 'D's – dotage, death and decomposition – so make the most of it. Maybe go part-time from work rather than stop completely, though make sure your colleagues know this: it's a bit awkward if you turn up the morning after your leaving party when they're all bitching about you and someone's already swiped your desk because it has a marginally better view of the industrial estate's car park than all the others.

### Trial and error

Retirement, at least in its early days, is very much a case of trial and error (it's only later on that it simply becomes a trial). As the man said, you should try everything once except incest and Morris dancing. Nothing is final* and none of your decisions need be permanent. You may even find yourself busier than you were before retirement.

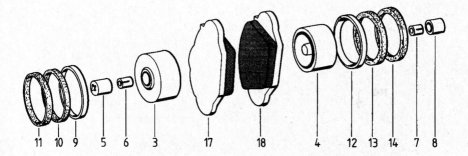

11  10  9    5   6   3        17        18      4   12 13 14  7  8

FIG 4•4 **TRIAL AND ERROR: FINDING WHAT FITS YOU AND VICE VERSA**

*Does not necessarily apply to BASE jumping, wingsuit flying and bull running.

# ⚠ The next chapter

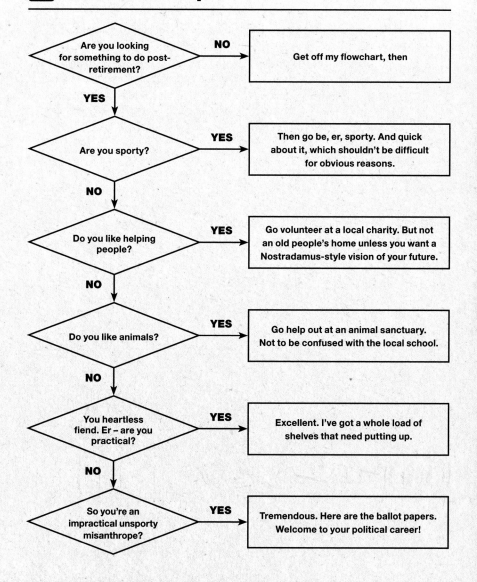

**Are you looking for something to do post-retirement?** — **NO** → Get off my flowchart, then

**YES** ↓

**Are you sporty?** — **YES** → Then go be, er, sporty. And quick about it, which shouldn't be difficult for obvious reasons.

**NO** ↓

**Do you like helping people?** — **YES** → Go volunteer at a local charity. But not an old people's home unless you want a Nostradamus-style vision of your future.

**NO** ↓

**Do you like animals?** — **YES** → Go help out at an animal sanctuary. Not to be confused with the local school.

**NO** ↓

**You heartless fiend. Er – are you practical?** — **YES** → Excellent. I've got a whole load of shelves that need putting up.

**NO** ↓

**So you're an impractical unsporty misanthrope?** — **YES** → Tremendous. Here are the ballot papers. Welcome to your political career!

# Residual value

Many wives will tell you that getting their husbands out of the rat race involves them bringing home less cheese: they get twice the husband at half the salary. With pensioners living ever longer (if you eat just alfalfa sprouts and drink kale juice, you might not live to 120 but it'll sure feel like it), making sure that financial provisions are in order is ever more important.

Even what used to be big numbers are going less and less far. Take a couple retiring at 65 with £1m worth of investments and withdrawing the standard rule of thumb 4% per annum. A combination of low interest rates and an average life expectancy of 85 mean they're now as likely as not to exhaust that money before they die. If that's not the most depressing thing you've heard today, you must spend your time listening to Joy Division, watching Ingmar Bergman movies or simply tuning into the news now and then.

You will therefore have come all the way down Acronym Alley, from when you were first married as a DINKY (Double Income No Kids Yet) via SITCOM (Single Income, Two Children, Oppressive Mortgage), GLAM (Greying, Leisured, Affluent, Married), WOOF (Well Off Older Folk) and now to SKIing (Spending the Kids' Inheritance).

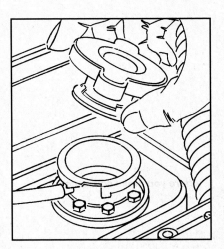

CAP YOUR SPENDING

TIGHTEN

REMOVE SLOWLY

FIG 4•5 **KEEPING A TIGHT LID ON IT: RETIREMENT EXPENDITURE**

# ⚠ Investment schemes/scams

If you're tempted to try and beat the odds by investing in a scheme that seems too good to be true – well, there's usually a reason for that. Run a mile (or perhaps walk/amble/shuffle a mile) from any of the following Maleficent Seven:

a) 'this great little real estate deal in Florida' your golf pro knows

b) the chance for your bank account to park £10m from the esteemed Mr Kunle Adebayo of Rivers State, Nigeria

c) 'my mate's got this AMAZING tech start-up idea'

d) anything to which the word 'pyramid' can be applied. Good pyramids – the ones in Luxor. Bad pyramids – all the others

e) holiday clubs. You'll be promised five-star luxury in the Caribbean. You'll end up with a half-finished hotel in Albania where the local dogs eat better than you do.

f) fine wine, gemstones, anything 'exclusive'

g) 'you're a lottery winner!' Usually in a lottery you didn't even know existed, let alone enter. Yes, technically it could be you. But it isn't. It's always someone else. Probably Derek down the road who you hate.

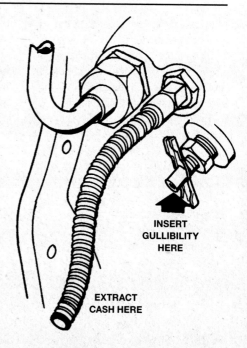

INSERT GULLIBILITY HERE

EXTRACT CASH HERE

FIG 4•6 **SIPHONING OFF YOUR SAVINGS**

## WARNING

*Beware the 40-40-40 scam, where you make someone else rich by working 40 hours a week for 40 years in order to retire on 40% of what wasn't enough in the first place.*

# Redline

The old adage that you should do something every day that makes you out of breath holds true in old age, perhaps more than ever before. And before you ask, smoking doesn't count. Have you seen the price of fags nowadays?

If you've been pretty sedentary during your working life, start off your exercise programme slowly. If you walk four miles a day starting from the age of 65, by the time you get to 90 you'll be thousands of miles away and no one will know where you are.

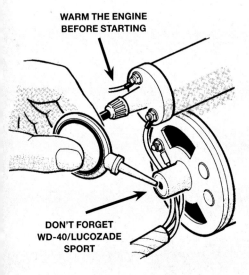

WARM THE ENGINE
BEFORE STARTING

DON'T FORGET
WD-40/LUCOZADE
SPORT

FIG 4•7 **GETTING ALL THE MOVING
PARTS IN WORKING ORDER**

## Health clubs

Maybe join a health club, but if you don't have the discipline to go there – or to actually work out once you're there rather than sit with a coffee and the *Daily Mail* – the only kind of pounds you'll lose are the ones in your wallet rather than the ones round your waist.

If you were active during your working life, then you'll find you no longer have to squeeze your workouts into the hour at lunch when everyone else in the whole world is either in the same gym or running the same routes through the park as you. Rest assured that they will still be suffering, even if you no longer come across them quite as often.

## Extreme sports

The over-70s now account for a fifth of all insurance claims for injuries caused by sports such as diving, mountaineering and skiing. They're:

**a)** breaking their hips while being hip
**b)** pushing 90 – mph
**a)** forgetting – to give a damn
**c)** going to bed at eight – in the morning
**d)** and the only death they're waiting for is the death metal concert to start. Rock on, old dudes!

#  Exercise for pensioners

### Cycling

Go to France and Italy and you can hardly move for septuagenarians whizzing up and down mountain passes on bikes that cost more than a small car. If MAMILs are Middle-Aged Men In Lycra, these guys are OATMEAL: Old-Aged Tough Mudders Experiencing Active Life. There are some things more humiliating for the younger man than being left for dead by someone twice his age on a climb through the Tuscan hills, but none spring readily to mind.

### Parkour

Also known as free running, it features in lots of pop videos and usually involves unfeasibly nimble people somersaulting over benches, leaping over walls and generally using the average urban landscape as some sort of SAS-style assault course.

Perhaps surprisingly, there is a version of this for senior citizens. Perhaps even more surprisingly, it's not a government plot to reduce the state pension liability. Parkour – OAParkour, perhaps, once a trendy Hoxton consultancy gets to rebranding it – helps older people with balance problems and also gets them to spend time outdoors.

### Triathlon

Swimming, cycling and running, all the way from 'sprint' distances (though think an hour or so rather than Usain Bolt) to the Ironman. Be sure to prepare properly unless you want (a) to start the race on a Sunday morning and end just in time to catch *Midweek* on Radio 4 (b) your triathlon experience to be more Marx Brothers than Brownlee brothers:

a) One pint the night before to settle pre-race nerves is good. Six more are bad, despite the scientifically unimpeachable grounds that beer = carbohydrates + water = ideal endurance preparation.

b) Keep your teeth clenched during the swim leg, unless you want each mouthful jointly sponsored by Castrol GTX and Thames Water Waste Management.

**A decent racing bike and proper energy gels will be a help. A Raleigh Chopper with a Turkish Delight taped to the handlebars less so.**

# Off-road capability

Walking, rambling, hiking, call it what you want – this is the section for you if your idea of a good day out involves any or all of the following:

a) An all-weather jacket whose design had more technical input from brainiac boffins than the Apollo space programme

b) A rucksack containing roughly half a ton of Kendal Mint Cake

c) A pair of those really useful but equally really annoying trousers that can be unzipped midway up the thigh to leave a pair of shorts exactly two inches shorter than a pair of shorts should decently be

d) Socks that claim to be blister- and odour-proof but which will inevitably leave your feet red raw and stinking of Gorgonzola after any walk longer than the amble down to the local shop

e) Hiking boots that either come from the same place as the all-weather jacket (see above) or which date from 1941, were worn by an ancestor during the Second World War, and retain water more effectively than a camel

f) An Ordnance Survey map enclosed in a transparent waterproof case

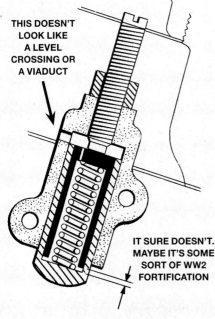

THIS DOESN'T LOOK LIKE A LEVEL CROSSING OR A VIADUCT

IT SURE DOESN'T. MAYBE IT'S SOME SORT OF WW2 FORTIFICATION

FIG 4•8 **WHEN ORDNANCE SURVEY MAPS GO WRONG**

### Nordic walking

This is when you stride purposefully up and down trails while swinging ski poles equally purposefully back and forth. If you had a pound for every smart alec who said 'you've forgotten your skis' as you passed them, you wouldn't have to worry ever again about funding your retirement (see Residual value).

# ⚠ Tips for hiking

**1)** Before you leave, inform someone of where you're going and what time you expect to be back. Make sure the person you inform doesn't have Alzheimer's.

**2)** Be aware of any dangerous animals, insects or plants you might encounter along the way. If you come across a bear and you're still in Britain, the mushrooms you snaffled half an hour before were slightly more magic than you thought. If you come across a bear and you're not in Britain, make sure you've brought a friend along who's just that little bit slower than you are.

**3)** Only pack necessities. You're going for a few hours, not attempting an unsupported crossing of the Empty Quarter. Water, energy bars, a whistle, a mobile phone, a map, a hat, sunglasses, sunscreen and a small first aid kit are essentials. Tolstoy-length novels, canned food, fire extinguishers, woks, hair gel and wellington boots are not.

**4)** You may be filled with an overwhelming desire to sing like Julie Andrews in *The Sound Of Music*. Do it.

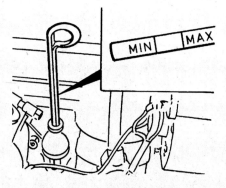

FIG 4•9 **COOLANT IS ESSENTIAL. ENSURE YOU ALWAYS HAVE SOME TO HAND**

**5)** Go at your own speed. Take in the scenery, take a few pictures, catch your breath. It's not a race. (Though if you keep being passed by people with numbers pinned to their chests, it probably is.)

**6)** Start early. Even in the rain-sodden, mud-filled, leaden-skied Mordor that is Britain in summer, mornings are cooler. Besides, you'll want to be back in time for *Countdown*.

**Hiking allows you to practice the four main types of exercise most pensioners need: strengthening, stretching endurance and balance.**

# Rolling resistance

If all that sounds too much like hard work, perhaps something a little more leisurely might suit sir?

You may think ball games are a thing of your past – few pensioners enjoy having red leather spheres hurled at their head by testosterone-crazed young cricketers or subjecting themselves to the usual football stream-of-consciousness 'yes over here on my head son release me release me give it wide to Gaz in the channel' – but two such games still pass muster in the Land of the Silver Fox.

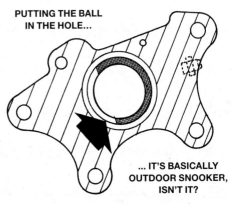

PUTTING THE BALL IN THE HOLE...

... IT'S BASICALLY OUTDOOR SNOOKER, ISN'T IT?

FIG 4•10 **GOLF. YELL 'FORE', SHOOT FIVE**

## ⚠ Golf, know the rules...

☑ **YES**, you can dress like a 70s pimp if you like (for some people – especially those who actually were once 70s pimps – this will be one of the game's chief attractions).

☑ **YES**, your wife will call herself a 'golf widow'. She used to mean it in anger. Now she means it in relief.

☑ **YES**, Mark Twain did call golf a 'good walk spoiled.' He also said 'whisky is for drinking, water is for fighting over,' so he knew what he was talking about.

☒ **NO**, it's not a good idea to be out on the course in a storm, especially if you're holding a metre-long piece of metal, which will conduct the lightning just so.

☒ **NO**, it makes no sense that most clubs ban jeans but will let you wear the most revolting shorts known to mankind.

☒ **NO**, you won't – even with the wisdom of old age – find your fellow golfers on a corporate awayday any less loathsome than you ever did.

# ⚠️ Playing bowls

Old people dressed in white and huddled together while concentrating furiously. No, not an amateur dramatic society's production of *The Pirates Of Penzance* or the local Ku Klux Klan meeting (in certain locales the two may overlap), but a meeting of the bowls club. Bowls is a close cousin both of curling, in which once every four years a quartet of formidable Scottish ladies win an Olympic medal by furiously sweeping the ice ahead of a large stone at which they shout Celtic imprecations, and pétanque, in which trios of Frenchmen from central casting pout, drink pastis and cheat, not necessarily in that order.

Bowls may look easy, but it's anything but. There's a ballet to the play, a subtle skill of judging the bowls' weight and the nap of the green. And don't assume that the genteel courteousness of the players means they're lax about rules. The players carry measuring tapes for a reason, and it's not in case they feel like a spot of impromptu DIY. They take this very seriously.

## Bowling's the ideal sport – a minute of exercise every 59 minutes of drinking and talking.

TRICKY TREVOR'S PARTY PIECE.
ROLLS THE BOWL SO IT...

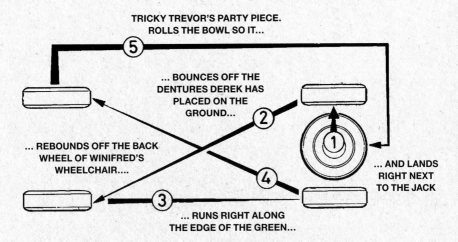

... BOUNCES OFF THE DENTURES DEREK HAS PLACED ON THE GROUND...

... REBOUNDS OFF THE BACK WHEEL OF WINIFRED'S WHEELCHAIR....

... AND LANDS RIGHT NEXT TO THE JACK

... RUNS RIGHT ALONG THE EDGE OF THE GREEN...

FIG 4•11 **THE COMPLEAT BOWLER: ANATOMY OF A SHOT**

# Pimping your ride

The words 'arts and crafts' may suggest nursery school or a short-lived architectural fad, but they're also something very popular with old people, either working at home or in community centres. Crafting helps both mind (keeping yours sharp and active) and body (manual dexterity in fingers and hands).

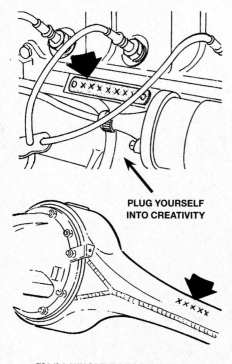

**PLUG YOURSELF INTO CREATIVITY**

FIG 4•12 **A WHOLE RANGE OF THINGS FOR YOU TO MAKE**

## 1. Knitting and crocheting

One of the most archetypal images of the granny, and with good reason. Give her some skeins and a couple of needles and watch her create magic – quilts, cushion covers and of course the old Christmas jumper. It's long been suspected that, contrary to popular belief, grannies the world over know their children and grandchildren absolutely loathe wearing a big woollen reindeer on their chest every Christmas – why else do you think they knit them? Think of it as your revenge for being sat in the corner all day with only Jeremy Kyle and endless cups of tea for company.

## 2. Photography

There's still a place for old-fashioned photo collages and scrapbooks in an era where 99.99% of photos are digital only. If you can get someone to use the printer with special photo paper, that is. Or if you can find the last outlet in the Western hemisphere that still knows what an old-fashioned roll of film is, let alone how to develop it. Actually, forget it. You may as well write letters on parchments with quills. Even those electronic photo albums, which used to scroll through hundreds of family photos with elaborate swipe transition effects, are old hat now.

## 3. Ceramics

Nothing says you're gradually but inexorably losing the will to live like a slightly wonky and badly painted coffee cup. In the movies it's all Patrick Swayze and Demi Moore doing pottery in *Ghost*. In real life it's, er, not.

## 4. Flower arranging

Your local church for a start will always need flowers, even if nowadays the blooms outnumber the parishioners. Whatever you want to say, you can always say it with flowers, particularly if you include deadly nightshade, a Venus fly-trap or a triffid in your arrangement.

## 5. Painting

Sit outside with a beautiful landscape opening up before you. Set up easel. Mix paints. Hold paintbrush vertical and squint knowingly at it. (This makes you look as if you know what you're doing, even if you don't.) Doze off. Wake with sunburn and a blank canvas. Repeat tomorrow. Or go to the life-drawing class instead, for obvious reasons.

**When painting or making something, you can find yourself and lose yourself at the same time.**

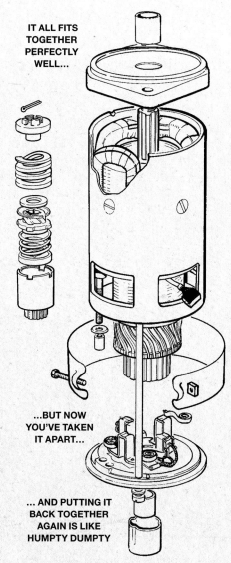

IT ALL FITS TOGETHER PERFECTLY WELL...

...BUT NOW YOU'VE TAKEN IT APART...

... AND PUTTING IT BACK TOGETHER AGAIN IS LIKE HUMPTY DUMPTY

FIG 4•13 **FULL STRIPDOWN AND REBUILD. THAT'S THE HAYNES WAY**

# OAP driving

More than 4m drivers in the UK are now over 70, the age at which licences must be renewed, and the oldest licensed driver is 107. There is no mandatory test to ensure that you are able to keep driving: the DVLA take your word for it, a rare example of public trust in the individual (well, there was self-certified mortgages once upon a time, and look what happened there).

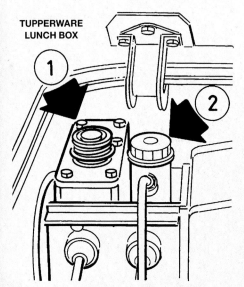

TUPPERWARE LUNCH BOX

HIP FLASK. GINGER BEER ONLY, OFFICER

FIG 4•14 **THE VALUE OF VEHICULAR VICTUALS**

### Driving tips

**a)** Young people have it too easy nowadays. Soft lives with no real danger. They're mollycoddled, don't you know? It's your civic duty to scare the bejesus out of them every time you take to the road.

**b)** Exchange whatever car you used to have for a light purple Nissan Micra, the Official OAP Car of Great Britain. Other drivers will instantly recognise you as a pensioner.

**c)** The Highway Code – that's a Dan Brown book, isn't it?

**d)** Windscreen wipers are overrated. In your day you used a cut potato to get rid of water and ice alike.

**e)** On any given road there's a speed slow enough to frustrate other drivers behind you but fast enough to prevent them from overtaking easily. It is your job to find this speed and stick to it. You will find it hard at first, but with a bit of practice you will nail it easily and ensure yourself many happy hours of hugely annoying everyone else.

**f)** Turn down your hearing aid so you can't hear other cars honking.

**g)** All policemen are about 12 and should be out catching real criminals.

**h)** Your reaction times will also deteriorate in old age. Luckily the number of young people on the road with excellent reflexes will balance this out. Sort of. In general. Probably.

**i)** Younger drivers will express appreciation of your driving by a variety of hand gestures, usually involving either the middle finger or a lightly clenched fist being moved back and forth. It's only polite to respond in kind.

**j)** The same younger drivers will then turn to their passengers and say in all sincerity that they're never going to get like you. They're never going to be driving around so slowly. What they won't know is that at your age you said exactly the same thing too.

**k)** Choose an automatic car if possible, though beware of models that come with electric parking brakes – they mean you won't be able to do handbrake turns and doughnuts.

**l)** If you're worried about your ability to drive, see a doctor. If you can't see him, your eyesight's probably not good enough to drive. If you can't read his writing, that's nothing to do with your eyesight – it's because he's a doctor and therefore uses hieroglyphics rather than letters.

**m)** Accidents don't count if (a) no one else was involved, (b) they don't take place on a public road. So wrapping the car around a lamp post, ending upside down in a ditch or totalling half a dozen other cars in the Sainsbury's car park are all non-events.

**n)** You may choose not to drive in certain conditions – in the dark, for example, or during bad weather. This means you will on average be able to drive around 27 minutes each year in Britain.

**o)** Sometimes the news gets it wrong. If you hear on the radio that a driver's going the wrong way up the A1, for example, and you're on the A1, you may think there's not one driver going the wrong way; there's thousands of them.

**p)** If the police come and take your licence away because you've been reported as unsafe, a tenner says it's a member of your family who's dobbed you in – and they've done so because they love you.

---

**If your neck is too stiff to look over your shoulder at junctions, don't worry about it. Just pull out after a suitable interval has passed and Use The Force.**

# Wear and tear

There's no escaping it: things slow down, hurt more or just plain fall off as you get older. There are two golden rules for all pensioners – never pass a toilet and never trust a fart – and for the gentleman can be added a third: never waste an erection.

There's a revealing test that shows people what it's really like to be old. They put earplugs in their ears, popcorn kernels in their shoes, wear gloves and ankle bands to mimic numbing and impaired walking respectively, and given glasses which restrict their vision. Then they're asked to walk down a corridor. It's a rare person who doesn't feel more sympathy for old people by the time they get to the end of that corridor.

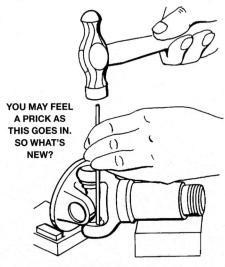

YOU MAY FEEL A PRICK AS THIS GOES IN. SO WHAT'S NEW?

FIG 4•15 **HIP OR HIPPY IN YOUR OLD AGE: HIP REPLACEMENT SURGERY**

**Your body will inevitably start to sag in old age. There's a reason that old men wear their trousers somewhere up around their nipples, and it's not because of fashion. On the plus side, you can have fun guessing what the tattoo used to be.**

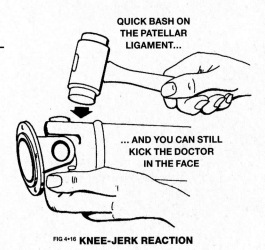

QUICK BASH ON THE PATELLAR LIGAMENT...

... AND YOU CAN STILL KICK THE DOCTOR IN THE FACE

FIG 4•16 **KNEE-JERK REACTION**

#  Common ailments

### Arthritis
Arthritis affects almost half of all pensioners. Remember those years of playing Monday night football or wearing high-heeled shoes? (Men may be less keen to admit to the latter than women are to the former.) They catch up with you in the end.

### Osteoporosis
Low bone mass is a problem for millions of pensioners, especially women. Falls can break bones much more easily than when in youth or middle age. Bones need calcium and Vitamin D, and can be strengthened by weight-bearing exercise (walking is good, powerlifting less so: there's a reason that Channel 5 show *The World's Strongest Man* but not *Britain's Strongest Pensioner*).

### Eye problems
Glaucoma, cataracts, macular degeneration: good eyesight is an inevitable casualty of old age. Now and then you may see a politician past retirement age reading a speech without glasses and wonder how he or she does it. What the TV doesn't show you is that the speech is printed in letters so large that the text can be seen from Google Earth.

### Hearing problems
Again, a fairly standard part of ageing, though also a good opportunity for tactical deafness in certain situations. My father-in-law is deaf in one ear. When I asked him which one, he replied: 'It varies.' Selective deafness allows you to potter in the garden while ignoring all shouts from the house to come and help with x, y and z.

### Teeth
Dentures are less common than they used to be as dental care has improved – and more people have used it – over the past few decades. With implants and bleaching, your teeth might even look substantially younger than the rest of you. Sometimes the only way for one pensioner with poor eyesight to identify another one in low light is to look for the lighthouse-bright flash of the pearly whites.

---

### Morning routine
1) Wake up
2) Grope blindly for glasses
3) Put glasses on
4) Open newspaper
5) Check obituaries column
6) If you're not in it, get up

---

# In-car processing

Ah, technology. The pensioner of today is the last generation to have lived more than half their life without the kind of modern digital technology that has exploded in the last 25 years. Even their children, those now in middle age who so derided the computer kids at school as the saddest of nerds, now use technology without a second thought, and as for their children – well, they find it more natural to finger-swipe left or right on a screen than turn an actual page of an actual book.

## Pensioners are striking back

You know all those acronyms people use on text to save time? Well, pensioners do that too, though theirs mean something different to what all those young people think.

| | |
|---|---|
| *ATD:* | *At The Doctor's* |
| *BFF:* | *Best Friend's Funeral* |
| *BTW:* | *Broke The Wheelchair* |
| *BYOT:* | *Bring Your Own Teeth* |
| *DWI:* | *Driving While Incontinent* |
| *FWB:* | *Friend With Betablockers* |
| *FWIW:* | *Forgot Where I Was* |
| *FYI:* | *Found Your Insulin* |
| *FYI:* | *For Your Indigestion* |
| *GHA:* | *Got Heartburn Again* |
| *HGBM:* | *Had Good Bowel Movement* |
| *IMHO:* | *Is My Hearing-Aid On?* |
| *IMO:* | *In Monday's Obituaries* |
| *LOL:* | *Lots Of Lumbago* |
| *MILF:* | *Meal I'd Like To Forget* |
| *OMG:* | *Old Man Groaning* |
| *OMMR:* | *On My Massage Recliner* |
| *POS:* | *Proud of Senility* |
| *TOT:* | *Texting on Toilet* |
| *TLC:* | *Totally Lost Continence* |
| *TTYL:* | *Talk To You Louder* |
| *TTYL:* | *Try Taking Your Laxatives* |
| *WAITT:* | *Who Am I Talking To?* |
| *WIWYA:* | *When I Was Your Age* |
| *WTP:* | *Where's The Prunes?* |
| *WWNO:* | *Walker Wheels Need Oil* |

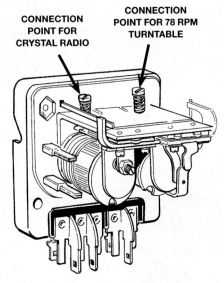

**CONNECTION POINT FOR CRYSTAL RADIO**

**CONNECTION POINT FOR 78 RPM TURNTABLE**

FIG 4•17 **PENSIONER TECHNOLOGY. STATE OF THE ART – FOR 1957**

#  Signs of the generation gap

**a)** Using the definite article for internet applications. 'How do you use the Twitter? Can I look it up on the Google?'

**b)** Photoshop. Putting little Donald Trump mouths where his eyes should be: why? Why would someone do that?

**c)** Putting an entire email text in the title bar. 'Can you bring me some milk and orange juice on the way home please?'

**d)** Ringing to check you've received their email.

**e)** When they ring your mobile, they always introduce themselves when you answer, heedless of the fact you have caller ID.

**f)** When you ring their mobile they always answer as if they don't know who's calling, heedless of the fact they have caller ID.

**g)** Selfies. Just don't get them, or if they do think they're a sign of the younger generation's raving narcissism. Which is a decent point, to be fair.

**h)** Waiting up to watch the weather after the news, even though any smartphone has a far more accurate and localised forecast available 24/7.

**i)** Handles are for doors, not for Twitter accounts.

**j)** Googling things. This works two ways. They will refuse to Google even the simplest thing, happily spending hours on hold to a customer helpline when the answer to their question is in black and white on the company's website. Or they will go the other way, especially when it comes to minor ailments. A pensioner with a mild cold and Google can convince themselves they have a medical history-making combination of cancer and tropical diseases in three minutes flat.

**k)** Using smartphone cameras. Some of Silicon Valley's finest minds dedicate themselves solely to improving pixels or ease of use. But hand your smartphone to a pensioner and ask them to take a picture – it'll be like one of those Victorian photo sessions when people in five layers of woollen clothing on a hot summer day had to stand stock still for four hours.

**Reading anything longer than a text message on screen. 'Can you print it out for me?'**

# Computer malfunction

Now, what was this section going to be about again? Oh yes, that's it. Memory, or more precisely its deterioration, is one of the banes of getting older. They don't call them the wonder years for nothing: wonder what day it is, wonder where my keys are, wonder where I left my glasses….

It's all to do with your left brain/right brain balance. There's nothing right on your left brain and nothing left on your right brain. (Actually, it's down to many things, including the decline in hormones and proteins, which protect and repair brain cells.)

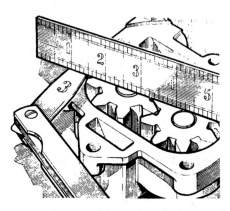

FIG 4•18 **CHECK GEAR MECHANISM FOR WEAR AND TEAR**

## ⚠ Mind techniques

**a)** Stay mentally active. Join a book club, read newspapers and magazines online, do puzzles such as Sudoku and crosswords

...............................................

**b)** Stay social. Talk to friends and family as much as possible.

...............................................

**c)** Exercise regularly. This increases the blood flow round the body (see above), boosts brain growth and reduces the risk of diseases such as diabetes, which can themselves contribute to memory loss.

**d)** Get plenty of sleep. Sleep replenishes neurons in the hippocampus, the area of the brain responsible for storing memories. This bit should be the least of your problems – you're retired, for heaven's sake! You can get up when you want and doze off in the afternoon too.

...............................................

**e)** Eat well. Fruit and vegetables contain antioxidants, and fish is rich in omega-3 fats. Both of these are good 'brain food'.

#  Perpetual motion

There are few things more soul-destroying than ringing customer helplines, especially when you've forgotten some or all the things they need to prove you're you.

How are you supposed to remember a password when you're always told not to write them down and to use different ones for various accounts?

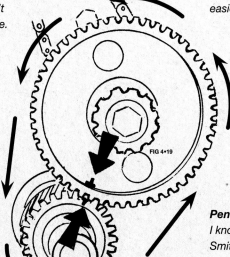

*Pensioner: is that the same one I use for my computer?*

*Operator: I don't know. You tell me.*

*Pensioner: Well, it doesn't matter because I've forgotten that one.*

*Operator: OK. How about your memorable date?*

*Pensioner: God, there are so many. But I can't remember any of them either.*

*Operator: Well, I have one on file here.*

*Pensioner: What is it?*

*Operator: can you give me your password, please?*

FIG 4•19

*Operator: Those are the rules. Maybe if we reset your password then things will be easier. So...*

*Pensioner: Why?*

*Operator: That's right! But you need to answer two questions before I can access your account.*

*Pensioner: I know this! Smith!*

*Operator: I was rather hoping you could tell me that. Why don't we try another security question? What was your mother's maiden name?*

# From SUV to supermini

The kids have grown up and flown the nest long ago. The house is not only a lot quieter without them but it suddenly feels very large too. So rather than rattle round an enormous space of which you realistically are only using a fraction, why not bite the bullet and downsize – move somewhere smaller (and cheaper, which with many years of retirement ahead is not to be sniffed at).

### Downsizing

Downsizing is never easy. Moving house is up there alongside divorce and serious illness as one of the most stressful things we encounter, and this is only exacerbated when the house you're leaving is one full of (hopefully) happy family memories (unless your family is the Mitchells of London E20).

**Downsizing is better in retirement than at work. 'We're downsizing' in retirement = 'we're moving to a smaller house.' 'We're downsizing' at work = 'you're fired.'**

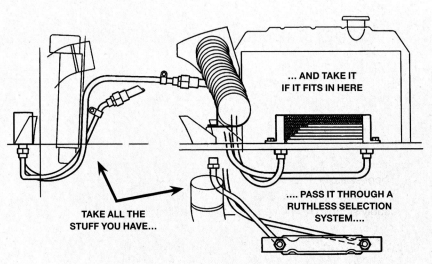

... AND TAKE IT
IF IT FITS IN HERE

TAKE ALL THE
STUFF YOU HAVE...

.... PASS IT THROUGH A
RUTHLESS SELECTION
SYSTEM....

FIG 4•20 **FITTING A QUART INTO A PINT POT: HOW TO DOWNSIZE**

#  Downsizing tips

**1)** Divide your possessions into three categories: keep, sell/pass on and chuck. Be ruthless. If you haven't used something in the last two or three years, are you really going to suddenly press it into service every day? Reserve special harshness for places like the kitchen, which are less likely to be packed full of sentimental items.

**2)** Start this process a long time before the move. An hour a day to work on a different filing cabinet or wardrobe will pay dividends. It'll also (a) make you slightly less alarmed at the sheer amount of clutter you've piled up over the years, (b) give you time to deal with the emotional rush of seeing things like your children's old toys again.

**3)** The sell/pass on section you can dispose of at – depending on their value – auction houses, car boot sales, on eBay, or via charity shops. The latter have probably stopped taking copies of *Fifty Shades Of Grey*, they receive so many. Probably best not to admit to having owned it in the first place, to be honest.

**4)** Hire a skip and fill it with all the things on the chuck list. It's surprisingly cathartic. Go for the biggest skip you can afford: it's amazing how quickly they fill up.

**5)** If you're especially indecisive, ask a friend whose judgement you trust to arbitrate on whether you should keep or bin certain items. Few people can resist this appeal to their inner Roman emperor, granted the power of life and death over an elderly Hoover.

**6)** Make sure your furniture will fit into your new house. Keep a copy of floorplans to hand and measure every big item, such as sofas and tables. The time to discover something doesn't fit is long before, not on the day when your removal men are becoming steadily less affable as you keep changing your mind about everything.

**7)** Mark your boxes clearly so you know what goes where. Give each room in your new house a number so you know what's what. You might also try coloured stickers as long as you're sure that neither you nor the removal men are colourblind.

# Up on blocks

When you can no longer live without assistance, it's probably time to consider a retirement home. Don't listen to the wags who refer to such places as Bedpan Alley, Chateau Coronary, Alzheimer's Acres or Catheter Flats. They'll be here one day themselves. (And besides, if you turn your hearing aid down you really won't have to listen to them.)

The retirement-home business is a varied and competitive one, so don't be afraid to shop around. With any luck you'll be here for a good few years, so it's important to get the decision right.

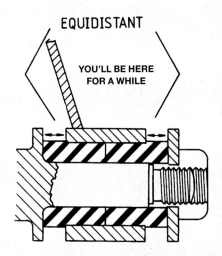

EQUIDISTANT

YOU'LL BE HERE
FOR A WHILE

FIG 4•21 **PUT DOWN THE STABILISING STRUTS.**

### 1. Is the food good?

Care homes, like armies, march on their stomach. It probably won't be Michelin star stuff, but nor should it be the kind of thing your dog would turn its nose up at.

### 2. How do the staff treat the residents?

Don't worry so much about residents yelling or moaning – that can be simply a distressing but unavoidable part of dementia – but check that the staff are helpful, polite and respectful. 'Sir,' 'Madam' and 'Mrs Smith' are good; 'blud', 'bruv' and 'pops' not so.

### 3. What does the place smell like?

Let's be honest – most retirement homes aren't ever going to be alpine fresh. But disinfectant (within reason) is better than the odours it's combatting.

### 4. Are the communal rooms full?

If so, this suggests that the residents enjoy each other's company and the home's activities are popular. A quiet home with every resident in their room may look peaceful, but if this is the case – as with schoolkids when they're too quiet – something might be up.

#  Retirement home truths

Once you've settled on your retirement home and settled into it, you'll find several immutable truths of assisted living:

a) If you pin a sign saying 'kick me' on a nurse's back, she will put one saying 'do not resuscitate' on yours.

b) The most valuable commodities are a car, a licence and a Viagra prescription.

c) If you're enjoying a walk and you come across ramblers saying they're looking for someone from your home, don't offer to help them search. Chances are your escape's been clocked and it's you they're seeking.

d) You'll get through so much alcohol-based sanitising cream that your hands will have to go on a 12-step programme.

e) If you find a suppository in your ear, you don't want to know where your hearing aid is.

f) If you hear the staff or your children discussing the 'youth in Asia', they're not talking about Japanese teenagers.

g) Try to take aerobics and yoga classes. Grunt, bend, twist and contort yourself for an hour. That's got your leotard on, at least.

**Remember all those years you spent changing your kids' nappies when they were babies? What goes around comes around. Just sayin'.**

**REG FLIPPED THE MASTER SWITCH WITH FIVE MINUTES OF CORRIE TO GO...**

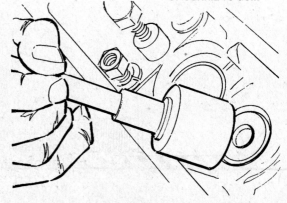

FIG 4•22 **... AND MADE HIS GETAWAY IN THE DARKNESS AND CONFUSION WHICH FOLLOWED.**

#  Fault diagnosis

| Fault | Diagnosis | Solution |
|---|---|---|
| You can't find your dentures and you have a pain in your backside | You're sitting on your dentures | Gently unclamp dentures |
| Your car won't start after you've been shopping | You're sitting in one of those kiddie ride cars outside the supermarket | Put £1 in the slot |
| You've seen this programme on the Food Channel a million times | You're watching the microwave go round and round again | Move either the TV or the microwave so you no longer get confused |
| No one you send letters to ever receives them | You're posting them in the red bin that's meant for bags of dog poo | Look for the red box with 'ER' on it. (This does not stand for 'Excrement of Rover') |
| Your most precious possessions aren't in your jewellery box | They're in your drinks cabinet | The solution is obvious |
| Your voice is beginning to give out on you | You need to talk less and use more non-verbal communication | Practice using your middle finger more often |
| Your doctor tells you to do more outdoor activities | Move a rocking chair onto the verandah | Take your naps in fresh air |
| Your hands hurt. You're not sure whether it's arthritis | It may be all those people who need a good slap | Slap all those people. Your hands may still hurt afterwards. So? |
| People say they're surprised to see you | They mean they're surprised to see you still alive | Continue to surprise them for as long as possible |
| The man from the DVLA has come to take away your driving licence | Get the man from the DVLA to go away | Run him over. That will both get rid of him and make his point for him. Double whammy |

# Conclusion

Retirement used to be seen more or less as God's waiting room – you worked, you dropped, and if you were lucky there were a few decent years in between the two. As we hope this manual has shown, the role of pensioners has changed and continues to change in deep and radical ways.

The pensioners' possibilities are almost endless. After four decades of living and working in a country where summer often comes and goes within 20 minutes, where the excuses for delayed trains are bewilderingly inventive and where you can set not just your watch but the atomic clock by the biennial failures of our national football team, you may even choose to go and live somewhere else entirely.

There are retired British expats all across the world, particularly in Europe. There are good reasons for this:

a) more sunshine than back home (that's not hard: it may be that Denmark is the only country in the world to think Britain is both cheap to live in and has good weather)

b) low-cost flights to allow your family to come and visit (this may of course be a mixed blessing)

c) the fact that English is basically the lingua franca of the world nowadays (though don't let this stop you asking locals 'do you know the way to the beach?' increasingly loudly and slowly). Remember too that you only need to know four words in any foreign language – 'my friend will pay'

d) many countries embrace the elderly rather than hide them away in retirement homes. Both Spain and Italy are actually run not by politicians but by an army of black-clad crones who sweep lintels, pinch children's cheeks, scold passers-by for rudeness and litter, and generally make sure that standards are upheld.

Whatever you choose to do, we hope your old age is both long and golden.

**Old age is when you realise that you will never be old enough to know better. And whatever it is, it's better than the alternative.**

## Titles in the Haynes Explains series

Now that Haynes has explained Pensioners, you can progress to our full-size manuals on car maintenance (advice on spares, repairs and high mileage), the *Retirement Manual* (the serious stuff), *Meteorology Manual* (for a sunny outlook), *Surfing Manual* (why not?) and the *Whisky Manual* (enjoying the spirit of adventure).

There are Haynes manuals on just about everything – but let us know if we've missed one.

**Haynes.com**